TRIVIA FOR SENIORS

365 Fun and Exciting Questions and Riddles and That Will Test Your Memory, Challenge Your Thinking, And Keep Your Brain Young

JACOB MAXWELL

TABLE OF CONTENTS

PART III: MIND GAMES FOR ADULTS

INTRODUCTION

According to a study, about 40% of people in the United States aged 65 or older have age-associated memory impairment. Unfortunately, as we turn into old age, there's a greater need to stimulate and engage our minds if we want to keep our brains healthy. However, most seniors tend to disregard this need and spend their days sitting in their lounges watching TV or engaging in unchallenging activities. Thus, forgetting names, losing keys, misplacing eyeglasses and missing important family events become the norm amongst people entering old age. It doesn't have to be this way.

It has been scientifically proven that seniors who regularly engage in stimulating brain activities or keep working their minds into old age can prevent memory-related problems and even illnesses like dementia and Alzheimer's. This is the reason this book was made- to keep your brain (or that of a loved one) active and intellectually engaged through activities such as memory games, brain teasers, and puzzles.

The exercises in this book, which range from simple riddles to problem-solving to trivia will work to delay cognitive function impairment, give your brain a powerful workout, increase visual perception and boost dopamine release.

If you're ready to get mentally fit, then continue to the next page!

200+ TRIVIA

FOOD TRIVIA

Question #1
American supermarket chain Whole Foods
is owned by which mega company?

Question #2
Ice cream mixed with soda is referred
to as what?

Question #3
Which country serves as the home of the largest
farm in the world?

Question #4
Coconut water can be used as what in the case of
medical emergencies?

Question #5
What is the official State fruit of New York?

FOOD TRIVIA

Question #6
What happens if you put a rotten egg in water?

Question #7
Immersing food in vinegar to prolong its lifespan
is known as what?

Question #8
Musician Prodigy of the rap group Mobb Depp
passed away after choking on what food?

Question #9
What is the only edible food that is said
to never spoils?

Question #10
A food product made from rolled oats mixed
with nuts and sweeteners is known as what?

FOOD TRIVIA

Question #11
Monterey Jack is a type of what?

———— ⚬ ❋ ⚬ ————

Question #12
A buffalo burger is made of which type of meat?

———— ⚬ ❋ ⚬ ————

Question #13
Which is the top-selling cookie in the United States?

———— ⚬ ❋ ⚬ ————

Question #14
Which treat has become synonymous with the celebration of Halloween?

———— ⚬ ❋ ⚬ ————

Question #15
What is the main ingredient in hash browns?

FOOD TRIVIA

Question #16
Munich's Oktoberfest is a celebration
of which beverage?

Question #17
Which type of pastry is boiled before it is baked?

Question #18
Donuts are traditionally sold in boxes containing
how many pieces?

Question #19
Baloney is a form of what?

Question #20
What is the primary ingredient in guacamole?

FOOD TRIVIA

Question #21

Fish fingers are also known as what
in the United States?

Question #22

Which is the largest food and drink company
in the world?

Question #23

Red Stripe is a popular beer brand that originates
from which country?

Question #24

Which beverage is advertised as being
"Sports Fuel"?

Question #25

Who was the former celebrity spokesman for
Jell-O pudding?

FOOD TRIVIA

Question #26
Henry John Heinz founded a company specializing in the production of which food product?

Question #27
Which country exports the most food?

Question #28
What do you call a vegetarian who only consumes chicken and fowl but no other meats?

Question #29
Who is the founder of the frozen-food industry?

Question #30
Which condiment is traditionally served with fried seafood in the United States?

FOOD TRIVIA

Question #31

In what year was the McDonald's Happy Meal created?

Question #32

According to legend, vampires are exceptionally vulnerable to which vegetable?

Question #33

What popular alcoholic beverage is made from fermented rice?

Question #34

Which American political figure was key in getting legislation passed to improve the nutritional value of food served in schools?

FOOD TRIVIA

Question #35

During the post-credits' scene in the hit movie "The Avengers", what dish are the superheroes enjoying together?

———

Question #36

What food would the fictional sailor Popeye consume to instantly increase in strength?

———

Question #37

Tacos are an increasingly-popular fast food that originated in which country?

———

Question #38

What is the main ingredient in makizushi?

———

Question #39

A snack made from marshmallows, graham crackers and chocolate are called what?

FOOD TRIVIA

Question #40
What is the name of the food that was miraculously provided to the desert-dwelling Israelites of the Old Testament?

ANSWER KEY

1. Amazon
2. A Float
3. China
4. Blood Plasma
5. Apple
6. It will float.
7. Pickling
8. Boiled Egg
9. Honey
10. Granola
11. Cheese
12. Bison
13. Oreos
14. Candy Corn
15. Potatoes
16. Beer
17. Bagel
18. 12
19. Sausage
20. Avocado
21. Fish Sticks
22. Nestle
23. Jamaica
24. Gatorade
25. Bill Cosby
26. Ketchup
27. United States
28. Pollotarian
29. Clarence Birdseye
30. Tartar Sauce
31. 1977
32. Garlic
33. Sake
34. Michelle Obama
35. Shawarma
36. Spinach
37. Mexico
38. Sushi
39. S'more
40. Manna

HISTORY TRIVIA

Question #1
Ulysses S. Grant appears on the front of which denomination of US. currency?

Question #2
Which fledgling network aired its first music video, titled "Video Killed the Radio Star," in 1981?

Question #3
Who was the first African American woman to be crowned Miss America?

Question #4
Who renamed the presidential yacht "Honey Fritz,"in honor of his grandfather, a former Boston mayor?

HISTORY TRIVIA

Question #5
Which president, the first to receive a Secret Service code name, was called "General," even though he was only a captain in World War I?

Question #6
Which F-word is used for the delay of a Senate matter by debate or procedural motions?

Question #7
Historically, parts from which animal were used to stiffen corsets?

Question #8
Who is the pre-Civil War author of a short story about a beating heart beneath the floorboards?

HISTORY TRIVIA

Question #9
Which founding father is known for his large signature on the United States Declaration of Independence?

Question #10
Name the second president of the United States of America.

Question #11
What was the name of the U.S. mail service, started in 1860, that used horses and riders?

Question #12
Who was the first US President to declare war?

Question #13
Who assassinated President Abraham Lincoln?

HISTORY TRIVIA

Question #14
Where was the very first Hard Rock Cafe
opened?

Question #15
Who painted the ceiling of the Sistine Chapel?

Question #16
How many U.S. Presidents have there been?

Question #17
What holiday was first observed under its current
name on November 11th, 1954?

Question #18
Who is the only U.S. president to serve more
than two terms?

HISTORY TRIVIA

Question #19
What is the world's smallest country?

Question #20
What famous actor became Governor of
California in 2003?

Question #21
How many people have walked on the moon?

Question #22
Saint Patrick's Day was originally associated
with what color?

Question #23
What is the name for the Greek goddess of
victory?

HISTORY TRIVIA

Question #24
Which one of the seven ancient wonders of the world is still standing today?

Question #25
Joseph Smith was the founder of what religion?

Question #26
What French sculptor created the Statue of Liberty?

Question #27
Who was the first president of the United States to live in the White House?

Question #28
In what year did World War II end?

HISTORY TRIVIA

Question #29
Which city is traditionally said to be built
on seven hills?

———— ⟨≫⟩ ————

Question #30
Who was the first man to set foot on the moon?

———— ⟨≫⟩ ————

Question #31
On September 24, 1906 President Theodore
Roosevelt established the first US national
monument. What was it?

———— ⟨≫⟩ ————

Question #32
Who was the first Roman Catholic to be Vice
President of the United States of America?

———— ⟨≫⟩ ————

Question #33
In 1893, which country became the first to give
women the right to vote?

HISTORY TRIVIA

Question #34
Malcolm Little was a civil rights activist better known by what name?

Question #35
What artist painted the late 15th century mural known as "Last Supper"?

ANSWER KEY

1. $50 bill
2. MTV
3. Vanessa Williams
4. John F. Kennedy
5. Harry Truman
6. Filibuster
7. Whale
8. Edgar Allan Poe - The famous piece is The Tell-Tale Heart.
9. John Hancock
10. John Adams
11. Pony Express
12. James Madison
13. John Wilkes Booth
14. Piccadilly, London
15. Michelangelo
16. 45
17. Veteran's Day
18. Franklin Roosevelt
19. Vatican
20. Arnold Schwarzenegger
21. 12
22. Blue
23. Nike
24. The Great Pyramid of Giza
25. Mormonism
26. Frédéric Auguste Bartholdi
27. President John Adams
28. 1945
29. Rome
30. Neil Armstrong
31. Devils Tower in Wyoming
32. Joe Biden
33. New Zealand
34. Malcolm X
35. Leonardo Da Vinci

SCIENCE AND NATURE

Question #1
A diamond will not dissolve in acid.
What is the only thing that can destroy it?

———————— ❦ ————————

Question #2
How big can be a lump of pure gold the size of a
matchbox can be flattened into?

———————— ❦ ————————

Question #3
True or False: Absolutely pure gold is so soft that
it can be molded with the hands.

———————— ❦ ————————

Question #4
How many miles can be an ounce of gold can be
stretched into a wire?

SCIENCE AND NATURE

Question #5
In 1982, in the first operation of its kind, doctors at the University of Utah Medical Center implanted a permanent artificial heart in the chest of retired dentist who lived 112 days with the device. What was the name of the first person who had this first operation?

Question #6
What is the only metal that is liquid at room temperature?

Question #7
Mineral deposits in caves:
The ones growing upward are stalagmites.
What do you call the ones growing downward?

SCIENCE AND NATURE

Question #8
True or False: Natural gas has no odor. The smell
is added artificially so that leaks can be detected.

―――――――

Question #9
In 1957, the Shipping port Atomic Power Station,
the first nuclear facility to generate electricity in
the United States, went on line.
In what country was this facility?

―――――――

Question #10
The damaged Chernobyl nuclear power station is
situated in which country?

―――――――

Question #11
What once covered 14% of the Earth's land area,
but by 1991 over half had been destroyed?

SCIENCE AND NATURE

Question #12
What is the approximate circumference of the earth?

Question #13
What prevents the earth's atmosphere from floating out into space?

Question #14
In which mountain chain would you find Mount Everest?

Question #15
Which part of a beetle's body is a skeleton?

Question #16
Which element is mixed with copper to make brass?

SCIENCE AND NATURE

Question #17
How many basic tastes can the human tongue distinguish?

Question #18
From which country did fireworks originate?

Question #19
Which lightweight metal is used in the manufacture of aircraft, cars and ships?

Question #20
Which composer wrote much of his finest music when he was deaf?

Question #21
What is the prefix denoting 'multiplied by 10 to the power 6'?

SCIENCE AND NATURE

Question #22
Which is the lightest of all the elements?

Question #23
In degrees Kelvin, what is absolute zero?

Question #24
Robert Oppenheimer is remembered for his work on which invention?

Question #25
How long does it take for light from the Sun to reach Earth?

Question #26
How many time zones are there in the world?

SCIENCE AND NATURE

Question #27
Which planet has the most moons?

———

Question #28
An octopus can fit through any hole larger
than its what?

———

Question #29
What is a group of whales called?

———

Question #30
What is the chemical symbol for table salt?

———

Question #31
At what temperature are Celsius and Fahrenheit
equal?

———

Question #32
What is the chemical formula for ozone?

SCIENCE AND NATURE

Question #33
What is the first organisms to grow back after fire?

———— ✹ ————

Question #34
What was the first planet to be discovered using the telescope?

———— ✹ ————

Question #35
Oncology focuses on what disease?

ANSWER KEY

1. Intense Heat
2. The size of a tennis court.
3. True
4. 50 miles long
5. Dr. Barney Clark
6. Mercury
7. Stalactites
8. True
9. Pennsylvania
10. Ukraine
11. Rainforest
12. 24,901 miles
13. Gravity
14. Himalayas
15. The outside
16. Zinc
17. Four
18. China
19. Aluminum
20. Beethoven
21. Mega
22. Hydrogen
23. Zero
24. Atomic Bomb
25. 8 minutes and 20 seconds
26. 24
27. Jupiter
28. Beak
29. A Pod
30. NaC
31. 40 degrees
32. O3
33. Moss
34. Uranus
35. Cancer

GEOGRAPHY TRIVIA

Question #1

With over 35 million residents, what is the most populous city in the world?

Question #2

Which is the only U.S. state's capital city with not a single McDonald's fast food joint?

Question #3

In which state is the historic Shinnecock Hills Golf Club located?

Question #4

Which Nordic country was first to give women the right to vote, in 1906?

Question #5

Catalonia is a region of what country?

GEOGRAPHY TRIVIA

Question #6
Which lake is the world's largest lake?

Question #7
What is the longest river in the world?

Question #8
Which is the only US state to produce coffee beans?

Question #9
What is the main dialect of Chinese spoken in Hong Kong by most of the locals?

Question #10
Sicily is the largest island in which sea?

Question #11
Which country has the most volcanoes?

GEOGRAPHY TRIVIA

Question #12
Which district in central Tokyo is particularly famous for its electronics?

Question #13
What is the official language of the Canadian province Quebec?

Question #14
What is the only sea on Earth with no coastline?

Question #15
How many school districts does Hawaii have?

Question #16
What mountains on India's Northern border are nicknamed "Snow Abode"?

Question #17
What island does the Statue of Liberty stand on?

GEOGRAPHY TRIVIA

Question #18
Which country (and it's territories) cover the
most time zones?

Question #19
What is the largest island in the Caribbean Sea?

Question #20
Brazil was once a colony of which European
country?

Question #21
Which U.S. state has the longest coastline?

Question #22
What is the name of the Capital of New Zealand
that is the southernmost national capital
in the world?

GEOGRAPHY TRIVIA

Question #23
In what mountain range is Mount Everest located?

Question #24
On which street was the New York Stock Exchange established?

Question #25
Portugal is bordered by what other country?

Question #26
What colorful body of water separates Saudi Arabia from Africa?

Question #27
How many time zones are in Canada?

GEOGRAPHY TRIVIA

Question #28
What nation produces two thirds of the world's vanilla?

Question #29
What U.S. state is the "Land of enchantment"?

Question #30
Which U.S. state is closest to Africa?

Question #31
What city is second largest in Australia?

Question #32
What city is second largest in Australia?

Question #33
The Black Forest is in what European country?

GEOGRAPHY TRIVIA

Question #34
What city is the capital of China?

Question #35
In the South, Hominy when ground is more popularly known as what?

Question #36
The world's deepest sea trench, about 7 miles below sea level, lies in the western Pacific Ocean, and is called what?

Question #37
The world's finest emeralds come from what country whose other major (legal) export is coffee?

GEOGRAPHY TRIVIA

Question #38

The steps of the New York public library are guarded by what animals (in statue form)?

———⟨ ✳ ⟩———

Question #39

What two countries come closest to any part of Japan?

———⟨ ✳ ⟩———

Question #40

In Japan there are two important cities whose spelling contains the same five letters.
What are they?

ANSWER KEY

1. Tokyo
2. Montpelier, Vermont
3. New York - The Long Island club was founded in 1891.
4. Finland
5. Spain
6. Lake Superior
7. Amazon
8. Hawaii
9. Cantonese
10. Mediterranean Sea
11. Indonesia
12. Akihabara
13. French
14. Sargasso Sea
15. 1 School District
16. The Himalayas
17. Liberty Island
18. France
19. Cuba
20. Portugal
21. Alaska
22. Wellington
23. Himalayas
24. Wall Street
25. Spain
26. Red Sea
27. 6
28. Madagascar
29. New Mexico
30. Maine
31. Melbourne
32. Saint Augustine, Florida
33. Germany
34. Beijing
35. Grits
36. Marianas Trench
37. Columbia
38. Lions
39. Russia and South Korea
40. Tokyo / Kyoto

DICTIONARY ENTERTAINMENT

Question #1
If all the common, everyday 2-letter words were listed in alphabetical order, what would be the first four on the list?

Question #2
What is the name of the Japanese art of paper-folding?

Question #3
What is the first animal listed in the dictionary?

Question #4
These two words differ in spelling by one letter: one means to influence, the other means to cause. What are the two words?

DICTIONARY ENTERTAINMENT

Question #5
Identify these words ending with "atic".
a. Extremely joyful
b. Related to the movies
c. Inconsistent

———

Question #6
What six-letter word related to music contains
five consonants and the letter Y?

———

Question #7
Which word, meaning confusion and noise,
comes from the name of a structure in the Bible?

———

Question #8
Can you write four different 5-letter words,
which begin with S, and ends with ING.

DICTIONARY ENTERTAINMENT

Question #9
What is the only word in the English language
that when capitalized it is changed from a noun
or a verb to a nationality?

———————

Question #10
What is the only 15 letter word that can be
spelled without repeating a letter?

———————

Question #11
What are the longest English words
without vowels?

———————

Question #12
What is the only English word that ends
in the letters -mt?

DICTIONARY ENTERTAINMENT

Question #13
What is the shortest complete sentence?

Question #14
What is the only letter in the alphabet that doesn't have 1 syllable?

Question #15
What are the only words in the English language with three consecutive double letters?

Question #16
What is the only state whose name is just one syllable?

Question #17
What do you call the infinity sign?

DICTIONARY ENTERTAINMENT

Question #18
What is the only word in the English language with all five vowels in reverse order?

⟡

Question #19
What is the oldest word in English language?

⟡

Question #20
What is the only capital letter in the Roman alphabet with exactly one endpoint?

ANSWER KEY

1. A: Am, An, As, At
2. Origami
3. Aardvark
4. Affect / Effect
5. a. Ecstatic b. Cinematic c. Erratic
6. Rhythm
7. Babel
8. Sling, Sting, Suing, Swing... others?
9. Polish
10. Uncopyrightable
11. Rhythm and syzygy
12. Dreamt
13. Go!
14. Letter W has 3 syllables
15. Bookkeeper and bookkeeping
16. Maine
17. Lemniscate
18. Subcontinental
19. Town
20. Letter P

GENERAL KNOWLEDGE

Question #1
An animal that lives part of its life on land and part in water is known as what?

Question #2
What fictional city is the home of Batman?

Question #3
Who did Jesus raise from the dead?

Question #4
What is the name given to the workplace and official residence of the President of the United States?

Question #5
What are the color of football goal posts?

GENERAL KNOWLEDGE

Question #6
Who was the President of the United States when
Al Gore was Vice President?

Question #7
Which tree's bark is used to produce aspirin?

Question #8
What country possessed the most-expensive
Christmas tree ever?

Question #9
What is the largest internal organ of the
human body?

Question #10
What was the term for the official policy of racial
segregation in South Africa until 1994?

GENERAL KNOWLEDGE

Question #11
As of the 2016 Olympics, which NBA player has been on the US Olympic basketball team a record number of times?

Question #12
How many stepsisters did Cinderella have?

Question #13
When did the Cold War officially end?

Question #14
What percentage of the surface of the Earth is covered by water?

Question #15
An equinox is marked by what notable occurrence?

GENERAL KNOWLEDGE

Question #16
Which liquor is made from the blue agave plant?

Question #17
Who came up with the three laws of motion?

Question #18
The theory that Earth's outer shell is divided into gliding plates over the mantle is known as what?

Question #19
Which element, previously used in the production of felt, lead to the expression "mad as a hatter"?

Question #20
How many gallons of milk does one cow produce in one day?

GENERAL KNOWLEDGE

Question #21
From which direction does the sun rise?

⸱⸱⸱⸱⸱⸱⸱⸱⸱⸱⸱⸱⸱⸱

Question #22
What is sushi traditionally wrapped in?

⸱⸱⸱⸱⸱⸱⸱⸱⸱⸱⸱⸱⸱⸱

Question #23
Which music diva lost both her brother and
husband to cancer in 2016?

⸱⸱⸱⸱⸱⸱⸱⸱⸱⸱⸱⸱⸱⸱

Question #24
What is the venue where tradition says the birth
of Jesus took place?

⸱⸱⸱⸱⸱⸱⸱⸱⸱⸱⸱⸱⸱⸱

Question #25
Which NFL player was incarcerated for engaging
in unlawful dog-fighting activities?

GENERAL KNOWLEDGE

Question #26
Who revealed to Andy the identity of the person who murdered Andy's wife in the movie "The Shawshank Redemption"?

───── ❦ ─────

Question #27
In what year did Christopher Columbus discover the "New World"?

───── ❦ ─────

Question #28
What has no electric charge, and is one of the fundamental particles making up an atom's nucleus?

───── ❦ ─────

Question #29
What is the name of the racing series that is a spinoff of "Super Mario Brothers"?

GENERAL KNOWLEDGE

Question #30

What part of the world do most Valentine's Day roses in the United States originate from?

Question #31

What planet is second from the sun?

Question #32

What is the maximum weight for a golf ball?

Question #33

International music sensation ABBA originate from which European country?

Question #34

What author finished writing "Paradise Lost" in 1967?

GENERAL KNOWLEDGE

Question #35
What bird is gifted to the singer on the second day in the song "12 Days of Christmas"?

Question #36
Who is the wife of the cartoon character Fred Flintstone?

Question #37
In what year were women first allowed to participate in the modern Olympic games?

Question #38
What is the first rule of Fight Club?

Question #39
Which popular singer is referred to as the "King of Pop"?

GENERAL KNOWLEDGE

Question #40
Who founded the game of basketball?

ANSWER KEY

1. Amphibian
2. Gotham City
3. Lazarus
4. White House
5. Yellow
6. Bill Clinton
7. The white willow tree
8. United Arab Emirates
9. Liver
10. Apartheid
11. Carmelo Anthony
12. Two
13. 1989
14. 71%
15. Equal day and night
16. Tequila
17. Sir Isaac Newton
18. Plate Tectonics
19. Mercury
20. 6 gallons
21. East
22. Seaweed
23. Celine Dion
24. Manger
25. Michael Vick
26. Tommy Williams
27. 1492
28. Neutron
29. Mario Kart
30. South America
31. Venus
32. 1.60oz
33. Sweden
34. John Milton
35. Turtle Dove
36. Wilma
37. 1900 in Paris
38. Never talk about Fight Club
39. Michael Jackson
40. James Naismith

100 RIDDLES

RIDDLE 1 TO 10

RIDDLE 1: The Dead Man

There is a dead man in the middle of a field, nothing is around him and there are no footprints of any sort. There is an unopened package next to him. How did he die?

HINT: As he approached the field he knew he was going to die.

RIDDLE 2: Guess The Pattern

One is to three as three is to five and five is to four and four is the magic number. What is the

---

pattern?

RIDDLE 3: How Is He Alive?

A man was born in 1898. He is still alive now at the age 33. How is this possible?

RIDDLE 4: Zoo Topia

What do you call a three-humped camel?

RIDDLE 5: I'm A Good Guy

There was a man who was born before his father, killed his mother, and married his sister. Yet, there was nothing wrong with what he had done.

Why?

RIDDLE 6: Going To The Mall

As I was going to the mall I met a man with seven wives, Each wife held two bags, Each bag held a mother cat, Each mother cat had six babies, how many people were going to the mall?

RIDDLE 7: Four Fruits

In a contest, four fruits (an apple, a banana, an orange, and a pear) have been placed in four closed boxes (one fruit per box). People may guess which fruit is in which box. 123 people participate in the contest. When the boxes are opened, it turns out that 43 people have guessed none of the fruits correctly, 39 people have guessed one fruit correctly, and 31 people have guessed two fruits correctly.

The Question: How many people have guessed three fruits correctly, and how many people have guessed four fruits correctly?

RIDDLE 8: Working Late

A man is discovered dead sitting at his desk, alone in the locked office. He did not commit suicide and there were no weapons in the room. The only clue is a sealed envelope on the desk in front of him. How did he die?

RIDDLE 9: The Last Place You Looked

How is it possible to always find what you're looking for in the last place you look?

RIDDLE 10: I Am Slim and Tall

I am slim and tall,
Many find me desirable and appealing.
They touch me and I give a false good feeling.
Once I shine in splendor,

But only once and then no more.
For many I am "to die for".
What am I?

ANSWER KEY
RIDDLES 1 TO 10

1. Failed Parachute

2. One has three letters in the word three has five letters in it five has four letters and four has four letters in it (if you try more numbers they will always come back to the number four: so, four is the magic number)

3. He was born in room 1898 in the hospital.

4. Pregnant

5. His father was in front of him when he was born, therefore he was born before him. His mother died while giving birth to him. Finally, he grew up to be a minister and married his sister at her ceremony.

6. One! As I was going to the mall I met a man...

7. It is not possible to guess only three fruits correctly: the fourth fruit is then correct too! So, nobody has guessed three fruits correctly and 123-43-39-31 = 10 people have guessed four fruits correctly.

8. The envelope glue was poisoned and when the man licked the envelope to seal it, he died.

9. :If you find what you are looking for then you would stop looking so it would be in the last place you look.

10. A Cigarette

RIDDLE 11 TO 20

RIDDLE 11: Birthday Gift

What did the hangman get his wife for her birthday?

<hr>

RIDDLE 12: Gallons of Water

You are right next to a river and have a 5-gallon container and a 3 gallon container. You need to measure out 4 gallons of water. How do you do it?

<hr>

RIDDLE 13: A Long Bridge

A large truck is crossing a bridge 1-mile long. The bridge can only hold 14000 lbs, which is the exact weight of the truck. The truck makes it halfway across the bridge and stops. A bird lands on the truck. Does the bridge collapse? Give a reason.

RIDDLE 14: The Cars Odometer

A car's odometer shows 72927 miles, a palindromic number. What are the minimum miles you would need to travel to form another? (a palindrome can be read both forwards and backwards, like "Kayak")

RIDDLE 15: Sisters

Sally, Lisa, and Bernadette are triplets. But Sally and Lisa share something that Berandette does not. What is it?

RIDDLE 16: The Puppy On The Internet

In 2000, a 40-year-old doctor told his son that when a little boy he decided to be a doctor by seeing a internet web site about performing a heart transplant on a puppy with a defective heart so that the puppy would live a normal life. I then thought that I would be a doctor so that I could help people in a similar way. What is the defect in this story?

RIDDLE 17: Lighter Than Air

Lighter than what I am made of, more of me is hidden than is seen. What am I?

RIDDLE 18: Of No Use To One

Of no use to one yet absolute bliss to two. The small boy gets it for nothing. The young man has to lie for it. The old man has to buy it. The baby's right, the lover's privilege, the hypocrite's mask. To the young girl, faith; to the married woman, hope; to the old maid, charity. What am I?

RIDDLE 19: On The Right Track

A man walking along a railroad track sees a train thundering at high speed towards him. Instead of immediately jumping off the track, he charges directly at the train for about ten feet and only then gets off the track. Why?

RIDDLE 20: Front and Back

What word is spelled the same way front and backwards?

ANSWER KEY
RIDDLES 11 TO 20

11. A Choker
12. You fill up the 3-gallon container and pour the 3 gallons into the 5-gallon container. You fill the 3-gallon container back up and pour it into the 5-gallon container. You empty the 5-gallon container and pour the 1 gallon left in the 3-gallon container into the five-gallon container. Then you fill the 3-gallon container backup and pour it into the 5-gallon container and you have 4 gallons.
13. No, it does not collapse. Because it has driven a half mile - you would subtract the gas used from the total weight of the truck.
14. 110 miles. (73037)
15. The letter 'L' in their names.
16. The internet did not exist when the doctor was a little boy.
17. An iceberg.
18. A kiss.
19. The man was on a bridge when he first saw the train, so he couldn't jump off the track immediately.
20. Racecar is racecar backwards.

RIDDLE 21 TO 30

RIDDLE 21: Think CAREFULLY

What three letters change a girl into a woman?

RIDDLE 22: Behead Me

As a whole, I am both safe and secure. Behead me, and I become a place of meeting. Behead me again, and I am the partner of ready. Restore me, and I become the domain of beasts. What am I?

RIDDLE 23: If You Can Buy 1 For $1

If you can buy 1 for $1, 14 for $2, and 145 for $3, what are you buying?

RIDDLE 24: An Extended Trip

Julie is going on an extended trip for three weeks. She lives in a remote area where there are frequent electrical power outages which can last up to three or four days. Julie has quite a bit of food in her freezer which would go bad if it thawed and then re-froze. She does have digital clock and a VCR which would flash 12:00 if the power went out. Unfortunately, the clock and VCR flash even if the power only goes out for a few seconds. What can Julie do so that when she returns home she will be able to determine whether the power was out long enough to thaw her food? Asking a neighbor whether the power was out, isn't a reliable option because the nearest house is half a mile away, and one house may have power, while another house may have no power. She won't be able to have a neighbor check on her house every day and has no one to house sit.

RIDDLE 25: The Prisoner

A prisoner is told "If you tell a lie we will hang you; if you tell the truth we will shoot you." What can he say to save himself?

RIDDLE 26: Hands

What can you hold in your right hand but not in your left??

RIDDLE 27: Donkey Crossing

A traveler came to the river side, with a donkey bearing an obelisk. But he did not venture to ford the tide, for he had too good an *. What is the missing word?

RIDDLE 28: Snoop Dogg

Why it is that Snoop Dogg needs an umbrella?

___

RIDDLE 29: The Alphabet and The Periodic Table

What is the only letter in the alphabet that does not appear anywhere on the periodic table of elements?

RIDDLE 30: Cogs, Tigs and Pabs

Some cogs are tigs.
All tigs are bons.
Some bons are pabs.
Some pabs are tigs.
Therefore, cogs are definitely pabs.

TRUE or FALSE?

ANSWER KEY
RIDDLES 21 TO 30

21. The riddle "Think CAREFULLY" is unanswered.
22. A Stable
23. House Numbers
24. One thing Julie could do is freeze a tray of ice-cubes and turn the tray of ice upside down in her freezer. When she comes home, she should check the tray. If the ice cubes are still in the tray, the food is safe to eat. If the trays are empty, it's time to clean out the freezer. She will have to make a judgment call if the ice-cubes are only slightly thawed.
25. You will hang me.
26. Your right elbow.
27. Asterisk = "Ass to Risk".
28. Because of the drizzle.
29. The Letter J.
30. False. Some cogs may be pabs, but not definitely all of them.

RIDDLE 31 TO 40

RIDDLE 31: First In Line

A Queen has twins by Caesarean section so it's impossible to tell who was born first. Now the twins are adults and ready to rule. One is intensely stupid, while the other is highly intelligent, well loved and charismatic. Yet the unintelligent one is chosen as the next ruler.

Why?

RIDDLE 32: Doctor

You go to the doctor because you're ill and he prescribes you with 3 pills and tells you to take them every half hour. How long do the pills last you?

RIDDLE 33: Two Grandmothers

Two   grandmothers,   with   their   two granddaughters;
Two husbands, with their two wives;

Two fathers, with their two daughters;
Two mothers, with their two sons;
Two maidens, with their two mothers;
Two sisters, with their two brothers;
Yet only six in all lie buried here;
All born legitimate, from incest clear.

RIDDLE 34: Black and White Riddle

The land was white the seed was black
It'll take a good scholar to riddle me that.
What am I?

RIDDLE 35: Not South West Nor East

Where is there is no south, west, nor east, and
weather not fit for man or beast?

RIDDLE 36: Water Gun

If someone robbed you in the shower, what would you be?

RIDDLE 37: Fred's System

Fred is listening to the raido when it suddenly stops playing. Nobody is with Fred and nobody touches the radio. A few seconds later, the radio resumes playing. How can this be?

RIDDLE 38: 5 Men

There were 5 men traveling down a road and it started to rain and 4 men sped up, the 5th did not, but they all arrived at the same place at the same time but all of them were wet besides the 5th, how?

RIDDLE 39: The Headless Man

A headless man had a letter to write; it was read by a man who had lost his sight. The dumb repeated it word for word; and deaf was he who listened and heard. Solve this riddle.

RIDDLE 40: Mailing A Valuable Object

Suppose you want to send in the mail a valuable object to a friend. You have a box which is big enough to hold the object. The box has a locking ring which is large enough to have a lock attached and you have several locks with keys. However, your friend does not have the key to any lock that you have. You cannot send the key in an unlocked box since it may be stolen or copied. How do you send the valuable object, locked, to your friend - so it may be opened by your friend?

ANSWER KEY
RIDDLES 31 TO 40

31. He is a male.
32. An hour because the first pill doesn't take 30 min. to take.
33. Two widows each had a son, and each widow married the son of the other and then each had a daughter.
34. An eye or an eyeball
35. The South Pole
36. An eye wetness.
37. Fred was driving his car through a tunnel.
38. He was dead in a coffin.
39. The letter in question is the letter "O". It is zero. The man had nothing to write. The blind could read nothing. The person who was dumb could repeat nothing. The deaf man listened and heard nothing.
40. Send the box with a lock attached and locked. Your friend attaches his or her own lock and sends the box back to you. You remove your lock and send it back to your friend. Your friend may then remove the lock she or he put on and open the box.

RIDDLE 41 TO 50

RIDDLE 41: Who Makes It?

Whoever makes it, tells it not. Whoever takes it, knows it not. And whoever knows it wants it not.

RIDDLE 42: Next 3 Letters

What is the next 3 letters in this riddle? o t t f f s s _ _ _?

RIDDLE 43: Thirty White Horses

Thirty white horses on a red hill, First they champ, Then they stamp, Then they stand still.

RIDDLE 44: What Does This Say?

WYISDERSOMENIMORORSIZASIZDENDERIS ORSIZ? What does this say?

RIDDLE 45: The Weird Camel

A camel travel a certain distance each day. Strangely enough, two of its legs travel 30 miles each day and the other two legs travel nearly 31 miles. Two of the camel's legs must be one mile ahead of the other two legs, but of course this can't be true.

Since the camel is normal, how is this situation possible?

RIDDLE 46: The Banquet

A great banquet was prepared for a Roman emperor and his courtiers. 22 Dormice, 40 Larks' Tongues, 30 Flamingos and 40 Roast Parrots were served. How many portions of Boiled Ostrich were served?

RIDDLE 47: MIRRORING CLOCK

A boy leaves home in the morning to go to school. Now he leaves the house he looks at the clock in the mirror. The clock has no number indication and for this reason the boy makes a mistake in interpreting the time (mirror-image).

Just assuming the clock must be out of order, the boy cycles to school, where he arrives after twenty minutes. At that moment the clock at school shows a time that is two and a half hours later than the time that the boy saw on the clock at home.

RIDDLE 48: Always & Never

It's always 1 to 6,
It's always 15 to 20,
It's always 5,
But it's never 21,
Unless it's flying.

RIDDLE 49: Stuck In A House

You are stuck in a house
You have four objects to use
You have a wooden chair, a ladder
A piano, and an axe.
The axe is rubber
What would you use to get out?? hint* you can't get out with breaking it
and you can only pick one object.

RIDDLE 50: The Light Bulb

There are 100 light bulbs lined up in a row in a long room. Each bulb has its own switch and is currently switched off. The room has an entry door and an exit door. There are 100 people lined up outside the entry door. Each bulb is numbered consecutively from 1 to 100. So is each person. Person No. 1 enters the room, switches on every bulb, and exits. Person No. 2 enters and flips the switch on every second bulb (turning off bulbs 2, 4, 6, â€¦). Person No. 3 enters and flips the switch on every third bulb (changing the state on bulbs 3, 6, 9, â€¦). This continues until all 100 people have passed through the room. What is the final state of bulb No. 64? And how many of the light bulbs are illuminated after the 100th person has passed through the room?

ANSWER KEY
RIDDLES 41 TO 50

41. Counterfeit Money
42. e n t they represent the first letter when writing the numbers one thru ten.
43. Teeth
44. Why is there so many more horses' asses than there is horses?
45. The camel operates a mill and travels in a circular clockwise direction. The two outside legs will travel a greater distance than the two inside legs.
46. 42. Each vowel is worth 2 and each consonant 4, so Dormice gives 22, etc.
47. The difference between the real time and the time of the mirror image is two hours and ten minutes (two and a half hours, minus the twenty minutes of cycling). Therefore, the original time on the clock at home that morning could only have been five minutes past seven: The difference between these clocks is exactly 2 hours and ten minutes (note that also five minutes past one can be mirrored in a similar way, but this is not in the morning!). Conclusion: The boy reaches

school at five minutes past seven plus twenty minutes of cycling, which is twenty-five minutes past seven!

48. The answer is: a dice. An explanation: "It's always 1 to 6": the numbers on the faces of the dice, "it's always 15 to 20": the sum of the exposed faces when the dice comes to rest after being thrown, "it's always 5": the number of exposed faces when the dice is at rest, "but it's never 21": the sum of the exposed faces is never 21 when the dice is at rest, "unless it's flying": the sum of all exposed faces when the dice is flying is 21 (1 + 2 + 3 + 4 + 5 + 6).

49. You use the piano KEYS.

50. First think who will operate each bulb, obviously person #2 will do all the even numbers, and say person #10 will operate all the bulbs that end in a zero. So who would operate for example bulb 48: Persons numbered: 1 & 48, 2 & 24, 3 & 16, 4 & 12, 6 & 8........ That is all the factors (numbers by which 48 is divisible) will be in pairs. This means that for every person who switches a bulb on there will be someone to switch it off. This will result in the bulb being back at its original state. So why aren't all the bulbs off?

Think of bulb 36:- The factors are: 1 & 36, 2 & 13, 6 & 6 Well in this case whilst all the factors are in pairs the number 6 is paired with itself. Clearly the sixth person will only flick the bulb once and so the pairs don't cancel. This is true of all the square numbers. There are 10 square numbers between 1 and 100 (1, 4, 9, 16, 25, 36, 49, 64, 81 & 100) hence 10 bulbs remain on.

RIDDLE 51 TO 60

RIDDLE 51: What Am I?

What is as big as you are and yet does not weigh anything?

RIDDLE 52: TWO CANNIBALS

Two cannibals were chatting as they had their dinner. One complained that he really quite disliked his new mother-in-law. What was the advice given to him by his companion?

RIDDLE 53: TO SHARE OR NOT TO

When you have me, you feel like sharing me. But, if you do share me, you don't have me. What am

---

I?

RIDDLE 54: A COWBOY

A cowboy rode into town on Friday, stayed three days, and rode out again on Friday. How did he do that?

RIDDLE 55: Purchased Item

The person who makes it has no need for it. The person who purchases it does not use it. The person who does use it does not know he or she is. What is it?

RIDDLE 56: NINE LETTER WORD

Which is the word in English that has nine letters and remains a word at each step even when you remove one letter from it, right up to a single letter remaining. List each letter as you remove them, along with the resulting word at each step.

RIDDLE 57: Eternity

From the beginning of eternity
To the end of time and space
To the beginning of every end
And the end of every place.
What am I?

RIDDLE 58: POWERLESS POWER

I can run but I can't walk, a mouth but I can't talk, a head but I can't think, a bed but I can't sleep. Who am I?

RIDDLE 59: Immeasurable

Until I am measured,
I am not known.
Yet how you miss me,
When I have flown!
What am I?

RIDDLE 60: Tasty

There was a green house. Inside the green house there was a white house. Inside the white house there was a red house. Inside the red house there were lots of babies. What is it?

ANSWER KEY
RIDDLES 51 TO 60

51. Your shadow.
52. So just finish your vegetables!
53. : A secret.
54. His horse's name is Friday.
55. A coffin.
56. 'Startling' is the word. Begin by removing 'l', which makes it 'starting', then take away the 't', making it 'staring', and so on - string; sting; sing; sin; in; and, I.
57. The letter 'E'
58. A river.
59. Time
60. Watermelon

RIDDLE 61 TO 70

RIDDLE 61: Man's Last Breath

What does man love more than life?
Fear more than death or mortal strife?
What do the poor have, what the rich require?
And what contented men desire?
What does the miser spend, the spendthrift save.
And all men carry to their graves?

RIDDLE 62: Puzzling Prattle

Two children, who were all tangled up in their reckoning of the days of the week, paused on their way to school to straighten matters out. "When the day after tomorrow is yesterday," said Priscilla, "then 'today' will be as far from Sunday as that day was which was 'today' when the day before yesterday was tomorrow!" On which day of the week did this puzzling prattle occur?

RIDDLE 63: Apples

A basket contains 5 apples. Do you know how to divide them among 5 kids so that each one has an apple and one apple stays in the basket?

RIDDLE 64: Pears

There are a few trees in a garden. On one of them, a pear tree, there are pears (quite logical). But after a strong wind blew, there were neither pears on the tree nor on the ground. How come?

RIDDLE 65: Sea Tales

The captain of a ship was telling this interesting story: "We traveled the sea far and wide. At one time, two of my sailors were standing on opposite sides of the ship. One was looking west and the other one east. And at the same time, they could see each other clearly." How can that be possible?

RIDDLE 66: Ship Ladder

A ladder hangs over the side of a ship anchored in a port. The bottom rung touches the water. The distance between rungs is 20 cm and the length of the ladder is 180 cm. The tide is rising at the rate of 15 cm each hour.

When will the water reach the seventh rung from the top?

RIDDLE 67: Small Hotel

13 people came into a hotel with 12 rooms and each guest wanted his own room. The bellboy solved this problem.

He asked the thirteenth guest to wait a little with the first guest in room number 1. So in the first room there were two people. The bellboy took the third guest to room number 2, the fourth to number 3... And the twelfth guest to room number 11. Then he returned to room number 1 and took the thirteenth guest to room number 12, still vacant.

How can everybody have his own room?

RIDDLE 68: Twins

Two girls were born to the same mother, on the same day, at the same time, in the same month and year and yet they're not twins. How can this

be?

RIDDLE 69: Wrong Street

A girl who was just learning to drive went down a one-way street in the wrong direction but didn't break the law. How come?

RIDDLE 70: Ouch!

I can be crushed to pieces but only if I am given away first, I can be clogged and attacked but that's usually my own doing. No matter how many problems I have, you wouldn't dare let me go. What am I?

ANSWER KEY
RIDDLES 61 TO 70

61. Nothing
62. The two children were so befogged over the calendar that they had started on their way to school on Sunday morning!
63. 4 kids get an apple (one apple for each one of them) and the fifth kid gets an apple with the basket still containing the apple.
64. At first, there were 2 pears on the tree. After the wind blew, one pear fell on the ground. So there were no pears on the tree and there were no pears on the ground.
65. The marines were standing back against the sides of the ship so they were looking at each other. It does not matter where the ship is (of course it does not apply to the North and South Pole).
66. If the tide is raising water, then it is raising the ship on water, too. So water will reach still the first rung.
67. Of course, it is impossible. Into the second room should have gone the 2nd guest, because the 13th guest was waiting in room number 1.

68. The two babies are two of a set of triplets.
69. She was walking.
70. A heart.

RIDDLE 71 TO 80

RIDDLE 71: Flopping on Sticks

I flop around on sticks and sometimes you cheer me as I do, I desperately need a white powder to do what needs to be done and looking at me you might wonder why I look like I am about to go swimming. What am I?

RIDDLE 72: Five Letter Word

What is the only 5 letter word that becomes larger when you add the letter "r" to it?

RIDDLE 73: What Am I?

I have a home and a big space, I have keys but I have no locks, I have lots of letters but I have no mailbox. What am I?

RIDDLE 74: Three and Four

What can you stick between a 3 and a 4 so that the result is more than three but less than four?

RIDDLE 75: Yummy!

Dark or white, sweet or bitter, sometimes I can be Belgian and sometimes I can be Swiss. What am

I?

RIDDLE 76: So Sweet!

I love sugars and treats, I am a little critter and I sound a lot like your Mom and Dad's sister. What am I?

RIDDLE 77: Hey, Doctor!

People say I put doctors out of business, sometimes I am sour, sometimes I am sweet, I can be eaten and can also be drunk. What am I?

RIDDLE 78: At A Restaurant

Hillary went out to dinner at a restaurant. She lost something very important. She looked everywhere but to no avail. Suddenly a beautiful waitress came up to her with the very thing she was looking for. What did the waitress say to Hillary?

RIDDLE 79: The Planet

You can find me in the Earth, Mercury, Mars, Saturn, and Jupiter but not in Venus and Neptune. What am I?

RIDDLE 80: Monkey Sitting On A Tree

There are two monkeys on a tree and one jumps off. Why does the other monkey jump too?

ANSWER KEY
RIDDLES 71 TO 80

71. A gymnast
72. The word "large"
73. A computer keyboard
74. A point, dot or period (3.4)
75. Chocolate
76. An ant.
77. An apple
78. Here's your Bill!
79. The letter "R"
80. Monkey see monkey do.

RIDDLE 81 TO 90

RIDDLE 81: Two Witches

What do you call two witches who live together?

RIDDLE 82: Golden Ticket

A box without hinges, latch, or lid. Inside a golden treasure is hid. What am I?

RIDDLE 83: Different Answers

What question can someone ask all day long, always get completely different answers, and yet all the answers could be correct?

RIDDLE 84: Hey, No Fair!

A magician was boasting one day at how long he could hold his breath under water. His record was 6 minutes. A kid that was listening said,

"That's nothing, I can stay under water for 10 minutes using no types of equipment or air pockets!" The magician told the kid if he could do that, he'd give him $10,000. The kid did it and won the money. Can you figure out how?

RIDDLE 85: Pick It

You pick it, you peel the outside, you cook the inside, and you eat the outside, and throw away the inside. What am I?

RIDDLE 86: Weird Family

There is a brother and a sister. The boy wants to visit his father in jail, and the sister wants to visit her mother in the hospital. But they both are not allowed in the jail or hospital. All they have is a gun. What do they do?

RIDDLE 87: What Does He Weigh?

There is a clerk at the butcher shop, he is five feet ten inches tall, and he wears size 13 sneakers. He has a wife and 2 kids. What does he weigh?

RIDDLE 88: Natural Family

A cloud was my mother, the wind is my father, my son is the cool stream, and my daughter is the fruit of the land. A rainbow is my bed, the earth my final resting place, and I'm the torment of man. Who Am I?

RIDDLE 89: Coffee or Soda

George, Helen, and Steve are drinking coffee. Bert, Karen, and Dave are drinking soda. Using logic, is Elizabeth drinking coffee or soda?

RIDDLE 90: Riddle Me This

I'm so fast you can't see me, though everyone else can see straight through me. I don't stop until the day you die. What am I?

ANSWER KEY
RIDDLES 81 TO 90

81. Broommates!
82. An egg.
83. "What time is it?"
84. The kid filled a glass of water and held it over his head for 10 minutes.
85. Corn
86. The boy shoots the girl, and then the boy goes to jail for attempted murder and the girl goes to the hospital due to her injuries.
87. Meat.
88. Rain.
89. Elizabeth is drinking coffee. The letter E appears twice in her name, as it does in the names of the others that are drinking coffee.
90. The blink of an eye.

RIDDLE 91 TO 100

RIDDLE 91: Bought and Stolen

I can't be bought, but I can be stolen with a glance. I'm worthless to one, but priceless to two. What am I?

RIDDLE 92: A Fox, A Goose And A Sack Of Corn

A man went on a trip with a fox, a goose and a sack of corn. He came upon a stream which he had to cross and found a tiny boat to use to cross the stream. He could only take himself and one other - the fox, the goose, or the corn - one at a time. He could not leave the fox alone with the goose or the goose alone with the corn. How does

he get all safely over the stream?

RIDDLE 93: Farmer Riddle

A farmer has twenty sheep, ten pigs and ten cows. If we call the pigs cows, how many cows will he have?

RIDDLE 94: Bus Full

There is a bus full of people travelling over San Francisco and no one gets off the bus throughout the journey. But when it gets to the other side there is not a single person left. How is this

possible?

RIDDLE 95: Gender Play

There is a word in the English language in which the first two letters signify a male, the first three letters signify a female, the first four signify a great man, and the whole word, a great woman.

What is the word?

RIDDLE 96: Never Eat

I have four legs but never walk I may be covered in flowers but have no soil I hold food three times a day but never eat a meal. What am I?

RIDDLE 97: Fragile Beauty

A very pretty thing am I, fluttering in the pale-blue sky. Delicate, fragile on the wing, indeed I am a pretty thing. What am I?

RIDDLE 98: Runs But Can Never Flee

It runs and runs but can never flee. It is often watched, yet never sees. When long it brings boredom, when short it brings fear. What is it?

RIDDLE 99: Up AND Down The Elevator

A man who lived on the top floor of a twenty-storey building had to go up and down daily for work, and of course, for food and the other necessities. On most days he could only ride the elevator to the fifteenth story, and he would have to walk the rest of the way. When it rained, however, he could ride all the way up to the twentieth story. Why?

RIDDLE 100: Proven Love

There was a man who wanted to prove his love to his wife. So, he climbed the highest mountain, swam the deepest ocean and walked the biggest desert. What do you think his wife said?

ANSWER KEY
RIDDLES 91 TO 100

91. Love.
92. Take the goose over first and come back. Then take the fox over and bring the goose back. Now take the corn over and come back alone to get the goose. Take the goose over and the job is done!
93. Ten Cows. We can call the pigs cows but it doesn't make them cows.
94. They are all married.
95. Heroine.
96. A table
97. I am a butterfly.
98. Time, which is often watched when you stare at a clock.
99. The man wasn't tall enough to reach the button for the 20th floor. He could only reach the 15th story button on the elevator. When it rained, he brought his umbrella, and used it to press the 20th story button on the elevator.
100. Nothing. She divorced him for never being at home.

50 MIND GAMES

MIND GAME 1 TO 10

1 THE MISTAKE

Look at the photo below. Can you find the mistake? Let's see how fast you can spot the mistake. Focus!

Can you find the the **mistake**?

1 2 4 5 6 7 8 9

2 THE WRONG DIRECTION

This time, you need to say if the word is located up in the box, down in the box, on the left side of the box, or on the right side of the box. Do NOT say what the word says. Ready, go!

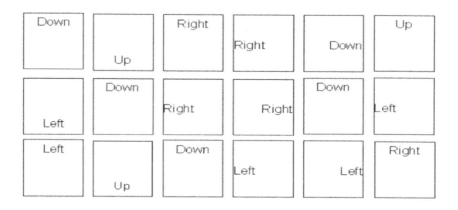

3 SQUARES, MORE SQUARES!

Squares be with you! Count how squares are there in this photo.

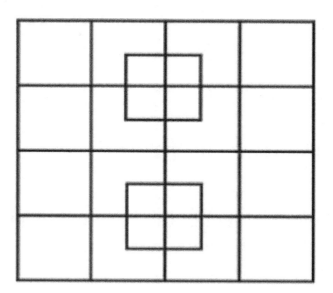

4 SQUARE AND FAIR

Look at the picture below. Count how many squares are there in this photo.

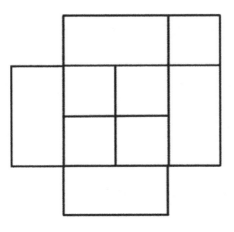

5 THE TRIANGLES

Look closely to this photo. Find all the triangles

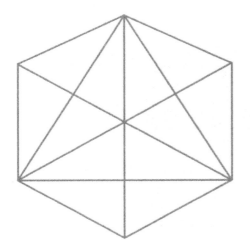

6 TRY THESE TRIANGLES

Look closely to this photo. Find all the triangles.

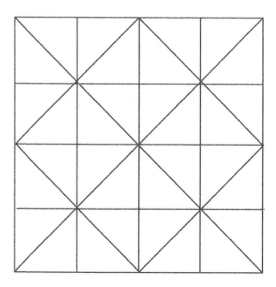

7 ANIMAL RESCUE

There are hidden animals in the photo. Find all of them.

8 HIDDEN ZOO

Find all the animals behind this photo.

9 The Face

What does this man say? Do you think you can trust him?

10 It's The Leg That Counts

Can you count how many legs does this elephant have?

ANSWER KEY

1. The numbers attract the eye & the reader may automatically find themselves checking those for a mistake. In fact, the error is hidden in the text that is "Can you find the the Mistake".
2. Just say the correct direction.
3. 40.
4. 11.
5. 25.
6. 96
7. 16 - Fish, Beaver, Tortoise, Elephant, Mosquito, Donkey, Dog, Snake, Swordfish, Cat, Mouse, Prawn, Hen, Crocodile, Dolphin, Bird Head)
8. 8.
9. No, because he is a liar.
10. 1, only the back leg.

MIND GAME 11 TO 20

11 Lucky Nine Horses

There are nine horses inside a squared fenced meadow. Can you construct two more square fences so that each horse will be in a fenced area by itself?

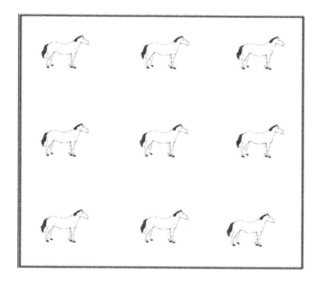

12 Chain Reaction

A man has 5 pieces of chain that must be joined into a long chain. He can open ring 3 (first operation), link it to ring 4 (second operation), then unfasten ring 6 and link it to ring 7, and so on. He could complete his task in 8 operations, but he wants to do it in 6. How does he do it?

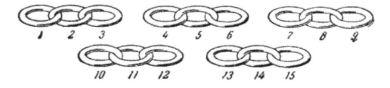

13 The Switch Challenge

Here is a light switch. Note the order of the positions. If the light is now at medium and it is switched 3922 times what will be the position of the switch?

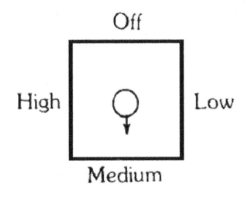

14 The Flags

A building is being prepared for opening. People are decorating the building with 12 flags. At first they arrange the flags 4 to a side, as shown, but then they see that the flags can be arranged 5 to a side using only 12 flags. How?

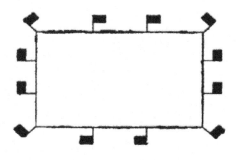

15 Pool Balls

You have 8 balls numbered 1, 3, 5, 7, 9, 11, 13 and 15. Select 3 balls and put them into the circles such that the sum of the numbers on them add up to 30.

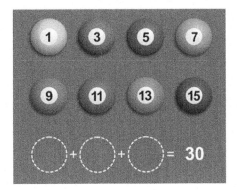

16 MATHsticks

Below is a little math equation, made of matchsticks that does not add up. Can you move just one match stick and fix the equation?

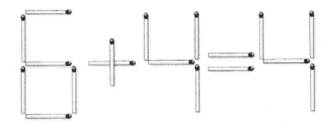

17 Crazy Cut

You are to make one cut (or draw one line) – of course it needn't be straight – that will divide the following shape into two identical parts.

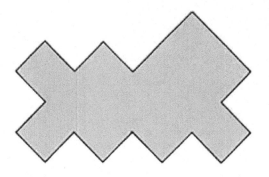

18 What's The Code?

Can you crack the unlock code for the lock using the 5 clues below?

CODE

Clue #1: 682 – One number is correct and well placed

Clue #2: 614 – One number is correct but wrongly placed

Clue #3: 206 – Two numbers are correct, but both are wrongly placed

Clue #4: 738 – None of the numbers are correct

Clue #5: 780 – One number is correct but wrongly placed

19 The Four Criminals

4 criminals are caught and are to be punished. The judge allows them to be freed if they can solve a puzzle. If they do not, they will be hung. They agreed.

The 4 criminals are lined up on some steps (shown in picture). They are all facing in the same direction. A wall separates the fourth man from the other three.

So to summarize:
Man 1 can see Man 2 and Man 3.
Man 2 can see Man 3.
Man 3 can see none of the others.
Man 4 can see none of the others.

The criminals are wearing hats. They are told that there are two white hats and two black hats. The men initially don't know what color hat they are wearing. They are told to shout out the color of the hat that they are wearing as soon as they know for certain what color it is.

They are not allowed to turn round or move. They are not allowed to talk to each other. They are not allowed to take their hats off.
Who is the first person to shout out and why?

20 Let's Go Swimming

A man wishes to reach the island in the middle of an ornamental lake without getting wet. The island is 20 feet from each edge of the pond (see diagram) and he has two planks each 19 feet long. How does he get across?

ANSWER KEY

11. Connect the midpoint of each of the four sides with four straight lines to form one square. Then repeat the procedure on this new square to form a square around the center horse.

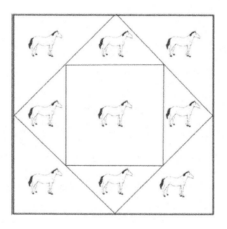

12. He opens all 3 rings of 1 piece (3 operations). With these, he links the other 4 pieces together. This will give a total of 6 operations.

13. The switch will be in the off position. After switching 4 times, the switch will return to its original position. So, 3922 / 4 = 980 with remainder 2. The switch will be at medium position after switching 3920 times, and at off position after another 2 switches.

14. Place 2 flags at every corner and 1 flag in the center.

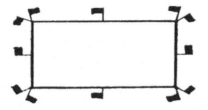

15. Rotate ball 9 to make into a 6. Place the balls 6, 11 and 13 to get a sum of 30. All the numbers are odd. There is no way to get an even number, 30, by summing three odd numbers together. At least one even number is required.

16. Solution 1: Make the equation 0 + 4 = 4, by moving 1 matchstick to make the 6 into a 0.

    Solution 2: Make the equation 8 – 4 = 4, by moving the vertical matchstick from the plus sign and add it to the 6 to make the 6 into an 8.

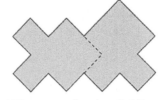

17.

18.   The code is 042.

Based on clue #1 and #2, we can say that 6 is not the correct number. Now we know that the unlock code does not contain 6 and based on clue #3, we know that 2 and 0 are correct numbers but in the wrong position. From clue #1, 2's position should be on the right. The code is ??2.

Based on clue #5, 0's position should be on the left. The code is 0?2. We have to find the missing number in the middle position. Based on clue #2, the middle number has to be 4. It cannot be 1, as the statement says that the number is wrongly placed.

19. Man 2 will shout first.

Man 3 and Man 4 will not be able to tell what color hats they are wearing since they cannot see the other men.

Man 1 can see Man 2 and Man 3 but is not able to tell what color hat he is wearing as Man 2 and Man 3 are wearing different color hats. So Man 1 will not shout out.

Then based on Man 1's silence, Man 2 is able to interpret that he (Man 2) and Man 3 are wearing different color hats. Since Man 3 is wearing a black color hat, so Man 2 knows that he is wearing a white color hat.

20. He lays the planks as shown in this diagram.

21 Bus Direction

In which direc-tion is the bus pic-tured below going? It is a school bus in the United States.

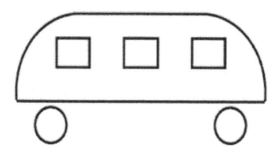

22 Two Squares

There are five squares formed by 12 matchsticks as shown in the figure. Can you remove just two matchsticks so that only two squares remain?

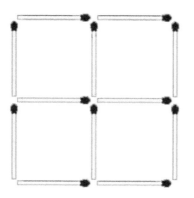

23 Teapot

If teapot A holds 32 ounces of tea, about how many ounces of tea will teapot B hold?

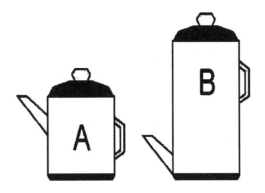

24 Holes in the Shirt
Look at the picture and guess how many visible holes are there in the T-shirt?

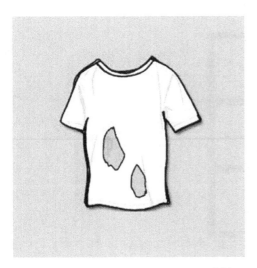

25 The Pyramid

Make the 10 coin pyramid on the left look like the inverted pyramid on the right by moving only 3 coins.

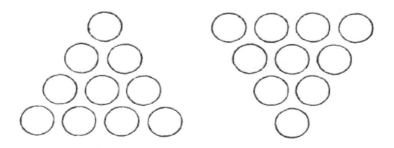

26 Fifteen

How can you place the numbers 1 through 9 in a 3×3 grid such that every row, column, and the two diagonals all add up to 15?

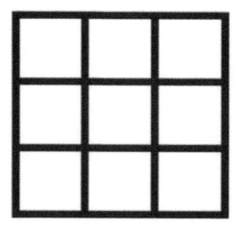

27 Twelve in All

Can you circle exactly four of these numbers such that the total is twelve?

I 6 I
6 I 6
I 6 I
6 I 6

28 The Dots

Look at the 9 dots in the image. Draw 4 straight continuous lines without lifting the pen from the paper and make sure that the lines pass through each of the nine dots.

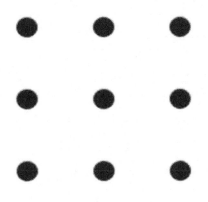

29 Parking Lot Number

The car is parked in which parking lot number?

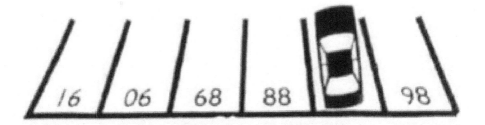

30 Squares Squares Squares!

How can you create 3 squares moving exactly 3 sticks?

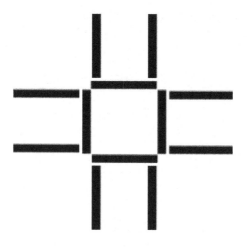

ANSWER KEY

21. The bus is going left. It is left-hand drive in the United States. Since you cannot see the door, the bus has to go left.

22.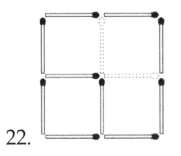

23. Teapot B will hold about 16 ounces of tea or half that of teapot A. The amount of tea that can be kept within each pot is determined by the height of the spout opening. The tea level cannot rise above the spout opening since any extra tea would merely spill out from the spout. A simple visual estimate would conclude that the spout of teapot B is approximately half the height of that of teapot A, therefore providing only half of the capacity, or 16 ounces.

24. There are 8 holes.

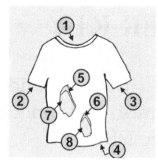

```
7 2 3 10
  4 5 6
   8 9
    1
```

25.

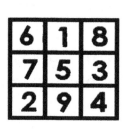

26.

27.   Turn the grid upside down and circle as shown.

```
9   1   9
    9   
9   1   9
    9   
```

28.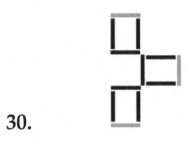

29. Parking lot number is 87. The numbers are upside down. Parking lots 86 – 91 are shown in the picture.

30.

31 Flip It Up

How can you flip the shape upside down by moving only two of the sticks?

32 Marine 101

Solve the equation.

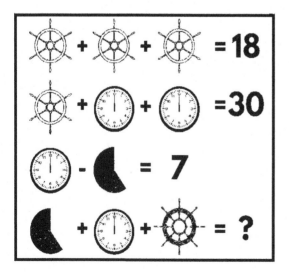

33 Food Challenge

How much is this?

34 Musical Instruments

Solve the problem.

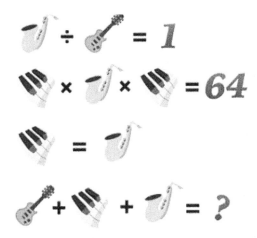

35 Multiplication Table

Find the value of each icon in the multiplication table.

36 Animals Gone Wild

Find the value of each icon in the multiplication table.

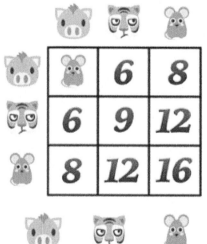

37 Without Lifting A Pen

Draw the following shape without lifting a pen and without drawing over other lines:

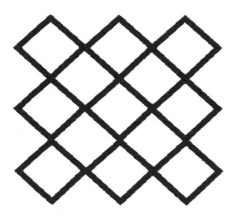

38 Rebus For You 1

Can you solve these visual word puzzles? Let your mind explore and you are sure to find the correct answers. Good luck!

funny funny
word word
word word

Not = Cent

39 Rebus For You 2

Can you solve these visual word puzzles? Let your mind explore and you are sure to find the correct answers. Good luck!

40 Rebus For You 3

Can you solve these visual word puzzles? Let your mind explore and you are sure to find the correct answers. Good luck!

mce mce mce

TEEF
FEET
TEEF

B U R poFISHnd

DAYSALLWORK

ANSWER KEY

31.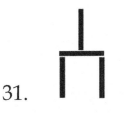

32. 24 (4+12+8)

33. 24 (Tacos value is 8.)

34. 12 (Guitar 4, Saxophone 4, Keyboard 4)

35. Volcano = 1, Statue of Liberty = 3, Rocket = 6, Race Car = 2, Ferris Wheel = 18

36. Pig = 2, Tiger = 3, Mouse = 4

37.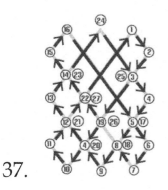

38. A bundle of nerves, Pinching pennies, The birds and the bees, Too funny for words, Not worth a cent (from left to right)

39. Adding insult to injury, Beat around the bush, No one to blame, Let the cat out of the bag, Take from the rich and give to the poor (from left to the right).

40. Three blind mice, Two left feet, Back rub, Big fish in a little pond, All in a day's work

41 Badminton Word Scramble

All of the scrambled words are badminton vocabulary words. Can you put the letters in the right order to spell the different words correctly?

FTNEI	
AHMSS	
ERSEV	
RSEAEEVCIAR	
ILTLOKHS	
CRELA	
ODPRHOST	
SOTODOHW	
AYRLL	
PHUS	
ECATRK	
ENT	
BEDIIR	
LNIEENTCER	
OLB	
URTCO	

ULFAT	
CEA	
AYRRC	
BDNAHCAK	
ELT	
SIELANEB	
NLE EDIIS	
DEVRI	

42 Find the Hidden Numbers

Find the numbers listed below. The numbers can be in any direction: backwards, forwards, up, down, or diagonally.

```
2  5  6  1  8  5  6  3  0  4  8  3  6  1  6
7  2  8  7  6  5  3  2  8  0  8  5  8  1  8
3  0  2  3  1  3  5  0  5  5  4  8  7  5  5
2  2  9  0  8  3  4  5  2  0  9  6  2  0  8
4  8  5  7  4  3  3  3  3  4  5  2  4  9  8
4  8  6  6  9  2  6  1  9  8  4  1  5  0  5
4  7  8  5  1  0  0  0  2  1  5  1  4  6  1
7  0  5  6  5  4  1  8  0  9  0  6  9  0  3
9  0  5  4  4  4  5  9  7  7  0  3  3  3  4
1  9  5  3  9  2  7  4  2  3  5  2  9  5  0
0  9  8  9  6  4  9  7  9  8  0  5  9  2  0
3  2  2  9  4  2  5  5  0  0  6  3  9  0  0
3  8  7  1  2  6  0  0  0  0  8  2  1  6  5
9  6  5  4  9  8  7  2  5  2  0  6  8  0  1
4  3  6  2  3  4  7  0  8  9  9  1  0  1  3
```

130456	410974	561280
150526	433334	567037
253060	436234	572855
270159	444791	588586
280858	454908	592884
286554	470085	642950
296684	481973	712600
322942	500043	870099
325326	520680	896497
399918	549872	991013

43 Word Sudoku (Medium)

These are played just like a regular sudoku, except that each of the digits is replaced by a unique letter. Each of the nine rows and columns, as well as each of the nine sub-regions, must contain one and only one of each of the nine letters.

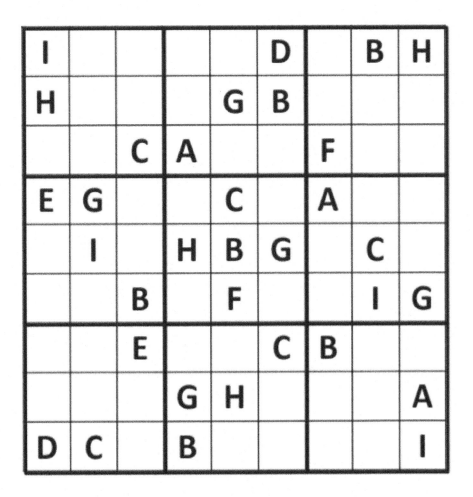

44 Jigsaw Sudoku

Jigsaw sudoku puzzles make a nice twist on the traditional format. Just as in a regular sudoku, the rows and columns must still contain one and only one of the digits. However, as you can see, instead of the usual regularly shaped subareas, known as nonets, the boxes are irregularly shaped. Just as in a standard sudoku, you may only put one of each of the digits in these subareas.

These puzzles can get your mind working in some interesting new ways.

1						6	7	8
9	6	7	2			5	3	
5	8			9			4	
							2	
		5				7		
	3							
	5			8			6	7
	4	6			7	8	1	9
8	7	9						3

45 Filled with Tea

Which one will fill up first?

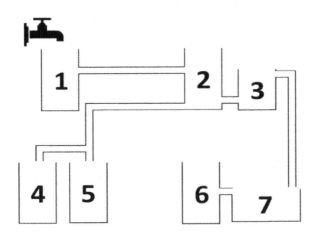

46 The Coffee Trick

Can you guess which cup of coffee gets to be filled up first?'

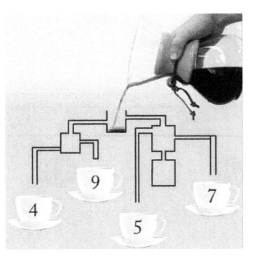

47 Visual Sequence Test

Which is the missing square?

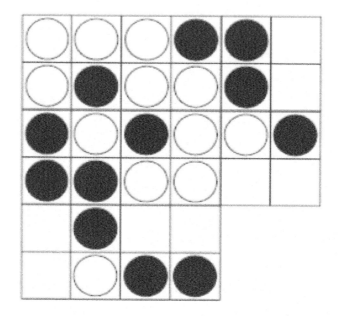

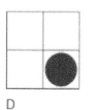

A

B

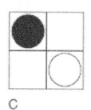

C

D

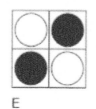

E

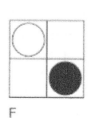

F

48 Missing Piece

Can you guess what the missing piece from the puzzle is?

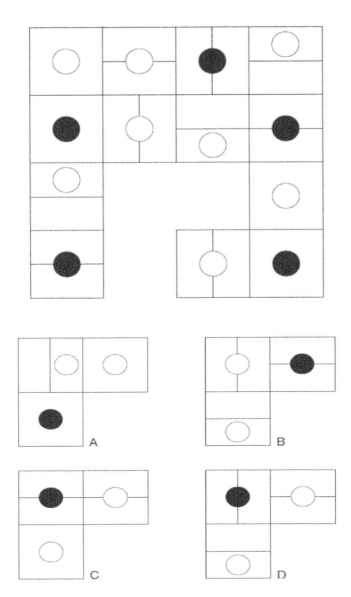

49 What's Next?

Which number completes the sequence below?

A.

| 6 | 10 | 18 | 34 | |

B.

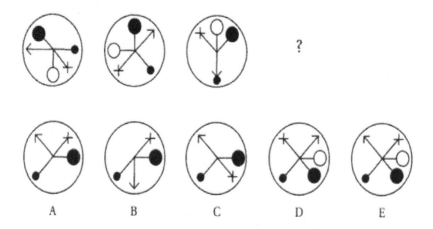

50 Circles Make My Head Go Round

Which circle should replace the question mark?

?

A   B   C   D   E

ANSWER KEY

41. Feint, smash, serve, service area, kill shot, clear, drop shot, wood shot, rally, push, racket, net, birdie, center line, lob, court, fault, ace, carry, backhand, let, baseline, side line, drive

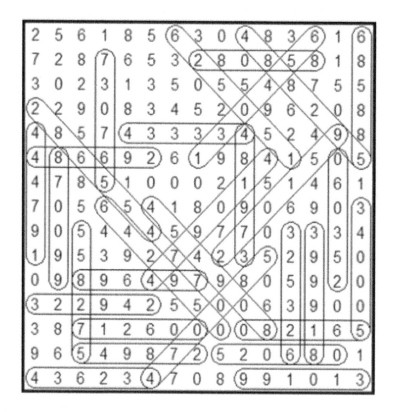

42.

I	A	F	C	E	D	G	B	H
H	E	D	F	G	B	I	A	C
G	B	C	A	I	H	F	E	D
E	G	H	D	C	I	A	F	B
F	I	A	H	B	G	D	C	E
C	D	B	E	F	A	H	I	G
A	H	E	I	D	C	B	G	F
B	F	I	G	H	E	C	D	A
D	C	G	B	A	F	E	H	I

43.

1	2	4	3	5	9	6	7	8
9	6	7	2	1	8	5	3	4
5	8	1	7	9	6	3	4	2
7	9	8	6	3	4	1	2	5
2	1	5	8	4	3	7	9	6
6	3	2	4	7	5	9	8	1
4	5	3	9	8	1	2	6	7
3	4	6	5	2	7	8	1	9
8	7	9	1	6	2	4	5	3

44.

45. Number 5

46. Cup Number 5

47. B. Looking across and down, only circles that are common to the first two squares are carried forward to the end square. However, they then change from black to white and vice versa.

48. D. The last two rows of figures repeat the first rows of figures in reverse.

49. A. 66. Working from left to right, double the previous number and subtract 2.

B. 6. The sum of the numbers in the lines of three going upwards equal the sum of the numbers in the lines of three going downwards

50. A. Each arm rotates a fixed amount at each stage.

CONCLUSION

Congratulations on going through this book! We hope that these exercises have helped to keep your brain young and healthy.

If you've enjoyed the book, then tell us about it on Amazon through an honest review. Reviews are the lifeblood of our endeavors and help us continue producing quality content, we're counting with yours!

"Anyone who stops learning is old, whether at twenty or eighty. Anyone who keeps learning stays young. The greatest thing in life is to keep your mind young." -Henry Ford

OTHER BOOKS YOU MAY LIKE

Exercise is undeniably important- even more so for seniors. Exercises and weight training into old age has been proven to be one of the keys to longevity and vitality. Many seniors feel intimated by exercising because of the risks and pain associated with it. Let me tell you that, with the right guide, just about anyone can begin an exercise routine and improve their physique! In Senior Fitness, I try to do just that- provide you with a guide that will test your level of fitness and offer you tailored workout routines and customizable exercises that will adjust to your needs.

If you're ready to get fit and feel at least 10 years younger, then get your copy of Senior Fitness today!

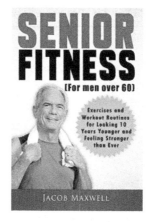

Find it on Amazon at: http://bit.ly/SeniorFitn